service

# service

## grant souders

T|P

TUPELO PRESS
North Adams, Massachusetts

Library of Congress Cataloging-in-Publication Data

Names: Souders, Grant, 1986– author.
Title: Service / Grant Souders.
Description: North Adams, Massachusetts : Tupelo Press, [2017] | Based on the
author's thesis (M.F.A.—University of Iowa, 2013). | Includes bibliographical references.
Identifiers: LCCN 2017000516 | ISBN 9781936797950 (pbk. original : alk. paper)
Classification: LCC PS3619.O874 A6 2017 | DDC 811/.6--dc23

Cover and text designed and composed in Centaur by Howard Klein.
Cover art: "Recycled Realities #48" by John Willis. Photograph of bale of a scrap paper on its
way to being recycled. Copyright © John Willis Photography (www.jwillis.net).
Used with permission.

First paperback edition: April 2017.

Tupelo Press
P.O. Box 1767, North Adams, Massachusetts 01247
Telephone: (413) 664-9611 / editor@tupelopress.org / www.tupelopress.org

Tupelo Press is an award-winning independent literary press that publishes fine fiction, nonfiction,
and poetry in books that are a joy to hold as well as read. Tupelo Press is a registered 501(c)(3)
nonprofit organization, and we rely on public support to carry out our mission of publishing
extraordinary work that may be outside the realm of the large commercial publishers. Financial
donations are welcome and are tax deductible.

*for CAS, JLS, KAS, VJS, and MBS and in memory of my father*

# Contents

service

# Naked

we enter the world naked
and the trees could care
less we haven't fucked well enough
else we would know better
it isn't dumb to love the woods
near your house so to walk
to and re-enter ourselves
one so alien I do love
in the coldness and warmth alike
because nature seems and is
and it is warm all summer
even the night we thought
it wouldn't but was and kissing
one another and after
death bridges of wood and steel
theoretical bridges
bridges drawn in mind there is one
bridge I swore I would never cross
enough bridges to deaths
and I do not speak ill of the dead
save the ones I did not like
and tongues wagging as the neighborhood
fills up with light certain days of season
we put ourselves together to drag
each other through one century
at a time there was time enough
enough and enough
winter and spring spring to summer
summer and fall fall and
life in a tree a bucket for shitting in
we didn't know it would be like this
how could we the first tree ever seen

the tree a ranger cut down and found
it to be the oldest living thing on earth
and his sadness
when we die how we put our mouths
inside each other's mouth
to speak on
the sun is good to see by
and we are getting better at things
even the bad ones

# Dweller

It was a name
given to me that called
me from sleep.

It was a bird.
A specific bird.
It was a cardinal that I had seen

pecking at my window a dozen times or more.
It was an average cardinal of average color
and, so, seemed to me familiar — like a cardinal, like each of them.

I turned my back on it
to go out to the east deck of the house
where a deer was rustling its neck.

It turned to me, as if to open
its mouth to speak to me.
*I am the way you know me to be.*

Other things wandered about.
Grass in the wind, for example —
is not easy to describe, so it did so itself.

When I walk, mind you,
where the deer have walked,
my mother tells me to watch for wildflowers.

They are lovely to see, to see and call out.
Don't step on the lovely things.
They grew lovely for a reason, she says.

How else?
I am asking you, how else the world descries
with and without reason.

Danger was everywhere and I found myself cautious.
But I saw the deer.
And the cardinal. And the wildflowers.

That is what brought me here, closer
to caution.

# Tracker

The wood bison took
to the woods

to the mountain
with numerous woods

to the one I live near
full of corpse and furl.

Once, I saw a mountain lion in the snow I've made.
It was soft glowing not fierce but that was ages ago.

Could you believe I called for valleys
in the plain?

I couldn't tell blue from hoofprint
shadow.  Or it was blue hoofprint shadow
I saw wherein the bramble I live near.
In tough thicket brush we've been missing
our callouses.  You have to have them
if you are going to go far, and you have to go
far to get them.

Occasionally there
is a fire to look at
and look by,
where we could've seen
the wood bison
where it went.

# Fisher

eye at the table at the map
scratching at the place the massacre
of you across

from the diner table with uneven legs left
thought thinking about the picture in Buell
I would conjure you

a precession of coal bounding over
over the train cars
like others we've managed what is

what is
this all beneath the clouds: clouds

get out the house
prowl the river
feet soaked & slipped over stone
we could've drowned & for the fish
a lightly tackled
moonbox

# Eater

I nouned
my mouth with
almond, automobile,
thicket thorn, mudgod.

It was those things
I was thinking.
Each small god.
I was thinking and looking.

There is a room in the bouquet.
There is a window in the room in the bouquet.
To go to the peeling back of things there is enough room
rough room, all silk and buzz.
I go out of.
Out of the window in the room in the bouquet there is a street.
The street is a banquet.
There are animals at the banquet.
Animals in rows.
There is a wolf with eyes that is an animal and a man that is an animal with eyes.
There are other animals with the man and the wolf in the street which is a banquet.
They are eating almonds and automobiles and thicket thorns and gods.
These things are in their faces where they eat them.
In their faces are the things they eat, but before they eat them, they hold them.
They hold them in their hands, paws, appendages.
If you'd like, we could join them.
There would be the things, then, in our faces where we eat them and hold them.

# Yard

We are in a house

as a lilac outside
window from housing
stray cat straying
into neighbor-yard
into little chips
bark scattered birch
leaf rote ground
a little play:

*Enter alarm*
comes awake

after extending, exiting

possessed in

what I thought, I saw

# Zenither

Tho tickled and trucked by sights
until now unforeseen, of course, how else
could we notice the pallid shells
of us we could climb up higher
there at the top of a neighboring roof
how I wish we

how I wish we
could levitate more than none
unaccompanied
by the naming of seconds, animals, whatever yet
we went out with simple intentions
to see elsewhere and thus confirm
our little profile

and a little farther
then further
we could touch a different piece
and I suppose we
do see so

# Arboretum

trees can
on hillside
by my house

drive down
I drove with
I think of

eye grove
the kick up
dust saw

as one approached

light
lighted dust
tufting

I left the willow
behind not because
it clanked too

hard against the window
its one window ours
or that it did not

hold the wren well
because
it did

what it does
& tho

I wont tell you how

I've missed it

blessed be the willow

# Horse

My mother taught me horses
after all
were broken

and I haven't lived long enough
for the perfect saddle.
We're broken

in the world, wordless.
If one can hold it in the mind
as a piece of air

which goes on
and the tongue pushes
the world out.

Like the curling of horses running
wildly.  Their hair tossing
in the push they've made.

And I find I am dumb.
I killed the horse
I rode to school.

# Auctioneer

I fear
amongst wintry air
air fronds and ear founds
to hope of
an axe blade:

*Let loose, wielding hand.*
*Give scape and page,*
*for I am December's dumb snow.*

To go south to go how
to go how come stunning,
thrilled thrush torquing:

*You came with a mind of heaven*
*supple gray, heather gray you wore thrill*
*thrills and death comes to breathe.*
*Even death comes to breathe.*

O — remember after our feet have dried
the place where they'd wet.

How yesterday held light as your skin
as distant suns happen
where light plays.  I said I saw
*A silly play.*

*Jugglers and such a pallid palette of gray.*
*Opening act where plucked temples from beneath the earth.*
*A stone head.*
*You lie in a ditch to dirge at all.*

What kind of alien
eats up ambrosian bouquets
only to lick?
*Nevermind alien. He comes, goes*
*as a tune to use and forget — what hymn*
*what hymn.*

But I own a little, and owe more,
am a thief in each house

Snow under boards

Then more sun

Snow under boards

# Shoveler

Well,
I dug out the well
hole where we had
suspected a leak
where the rock, unearthed,
grew a hole
innocent without voice,
calling attention
to earth and fled

When will there be a new star
all the time

and everywhere
the best thing we
can do is make
the hole evident
before we go

# What

All the while synapse sparking
*and if*
*and then*
*water like promise*
*patience.*

*What* is essential
as *what hisses in the lemongrass,*
*living as gravity acquiring silt.*

The exact gravity of particle.  A time ago
every mass scattered.  *A* condensed.
Leaf blew off sill
eternally, is drawn nearer to some still.
We're struck.

What is hollow?
*The mouth.*
*The mouth of rivers and of spells.*
*Dry spells where the river is riverless.*

The body craves air.
The air carves the earth.
*Grasps at it.*

Lemongrass.
Lilac.
Falling.

The gravity that is
absolutely ours.

We say *We* and then *they*,
*who we called them*
*are on another peak. So distant...*

We chase, they continue,
and the hollow leaves
itself.

We cannot cross the river of transfiguration.

What is waiting and passing?
*Lemongrass*                    *Lilac*

Look.
The reddish pith,
the yellow, brittle palm.
The sun expands.
Of everything drawn,
a diagram of light for us.
A loop drawn out.
A where
where we walked at noon,
where there was
a sense of it, remember?
Remember what.

# Lightbelt

this slop tick in hayfield
in whips of lily down
cottonwood thru light

belting my eye
musk talk where we were there
tho without pail

nothing to fill
lip writ limb and pathetic
some ghostcharm we are

what it is is how
headlight thrills an aspen grove
then thrill stomped out

by July all the time
here it is burden all the time
so call burden another name

and for that matter
need when slips of creek
plough new

when there's nothing to say
nothing speaks like paper folds
we'd nailed to the ceiling

we stopped again
at the aspen sight
let nothing be but be

# Lighthouse

Just now, I had the urge to spill across the table
flips of brief light that could be seen from
tossing bits of white linen into a bowl.

It is filled with fruit, some old and scattering
its smell as the light hit pierced, the smell.
Too much of everything is hardly enough.

Give me more.
I say this with my hands.
My palm is a bed for what ocean?
What psalm?
Give salt and nothing else
but a solace in time's lisp.

Less now.  Give me a cup and a shelf
where I am to place a cup and shells and the
gathered fur of years and years' dust
and dusks filling in the bedplate.
Don't we share thirst and know nothing of years?
How else is given but gift.
My mouth is at the cup you had only just held,
now you talk and the light. I miss
so much so often.

For example, what is lost.

There, where we commune
with the sharpness of skylight?
A we is set into motion.
Rather dropped and how else
Did we arrive?

If so, how so?
I saw rain coming
then it fell.

My palms are calloused from days digging holes for fenceposts.

I break to look to ask —

How far can you carry your house?

# Inheritor

we sang a borrowed song
sang it
to the canyon and the canyon
speaks us back

I want a scene that begins with a bird
the grackle in the big tree
that spooks out then

the cardinal tapping at the window
beak fitted for what to feed on

it wants to fill its mouth
as much as I want

all there is
is under consideration

# Petal

Petal when it's
the petal you can't see
and suddenly, the petaling flowers
makes a crown of them.
A crown for the mound it was given to.

Then Jacob wrestled the angel and the pale
hoods of the nuns as they look on at Jacob
from the ones you can see, not their faces
but their hoods.

Their faces are hidden as some petals are hidden
and we are one of the nuns wearing a hood, a crown.

That the petals are crushed
back into the earth by the weight of Jacob
and of the nuns, the sermon is over.

The petals more pigment and everything becoming
out of green.

Out of green, red.

The petal crushes by weight of the petal.

Some crowns are allotted eternity.

# Pairer

there is an insect boring its children
into dark

the desk my hand built
the tree built

a home for the borer and houser

you touched water as though to feel
your own disruption

there was a crow's nest
where I saw nothing but water

it turns out
I've said nothing
at last

# Chair

there is the blue chair I sat
on to drink the air and about me

food I asked my father
should I fear god

he answered yes
as I sat on the blue chair

he is dead now
as tho I could remember him and his

chair at the slanted breakfast table
we'd folded a dispelling envelope beneath a leg

weren't we warned or warranted
for something like this

all year long we ate fish and pickled fish
and grew tired and sleep undertook us to

a carpenter's oak splitting because
there was that storm inside itself

let me go under, blanketed
tomorrow I build chairs

and you admired the oak
that I planed still warm

and you in your dress
looking at what you held

you let me go to
what I do next

# Creek

Methodically, we
have set out on this venture
of various discernible birds.
A ruddy flock swung.
Meanwhile, the globe spinning
as we are of it
wrapping our dead in cloth
spun round a spooling procession.
When to think globe, it is of us.

The cup is graspable.
Beside me, the cup. The pallid
cup just within reach.
As I think of the roof
of my home, its gray gutters
because at this time of year
it is the present as it is
and there hasn't been rain.
This table cloth peaked with light.
The cup is graspable.
Suddenly, strange music.
From the neighbors?
Are they also home?

If when you go to Pickett Creek,
and having gone there you think back on it.
Or back in it,
That water, there, flecked with light
and the memory of it.
You hold things.
The water flecked
flocks of sunlight
in the way they hold
each other.

Stone holds not the water
but the river.  River over stone
within this eddying
pool we've now found
each other in.

Inside the train cabin there is a rocking
of hunger, of the child
with his hood pulled close, his thumbs
together, looking out. How
the window itself, by the world through the world
which shifts without me.
Still the cloudy glasses out my senses
(I too am looking out)
of passing trees, the clouded trees.
The train goes its way of being
in abandon. It abandons to and from
and there it is perpetually.
Perpetually, I see half
what the train sees
my eye, the train halves the world
outside the train what is
what wonders then Wimbley.

Wimbley, I say to the chlid.
We are here in Wimbley
all stepping off the train,
are at the train station
thumbing gestures stilling
breeze the atmosphere
growing between us
a pale veil.

# Painter

I am sleeping in a rowboat
where Titian painted the back of my skull.
I parted with him at the beginning of a different millennium.
The millennium was a river. Eventually it was dammed.
Until recently, I suppose because Titian and I parted
and I am only now remembering our parting, I had not desired
to see his painting on the back of my skull.
Several steps were required to unveil what may or may not
be a masterpiece.
First, I sharpened a scalpel and phoned a friend.
He agreed. Some things must be revealed and others concealed.
This was a case of the former.
Before tooling the scalpel, he shaved my head. Down to the scalp
like a ballpoint pen, or the surface of some misshapen moon
in a different system. One we won't find for years.
We did not speak of Titian or of that other millennium.
Once my barren scalp was exposed, the scalpel was taken to hand.
He made his incision with nervousness. But he knew words
like *must*. He cut a small rectangle and peeled away the skin.
I asked him what he saw. There was a pause. He was contemplating
or so I assumed. He said he saw only blood and the faint yellowed
white of skull and its minute fractures.
There is no painting here, he said.
Only you and what I've done.

# Tiller

I turned up a bone in the yard as yellow as I thought it could be.
I was tilling up then for what I thought was the future
for what I thought was tomorrow, but instead came later to me
and the sun is beyond the farm house.
To lessen what I can say of it. Over there, there are trees
But I am tilling the land and it has nothing
to do with the trees. That tree, over there, that I am pointing
at. You will know when you see it I will know that.
Then we both can go ahead and sleep and sleep
and dream or sleep and not wake like a wall
facing a stream. Where there are also trees but not like
that tree, the one I had told you about. And is that tree
so big or am I? As a pebble passing time over the Atlantic,
my breath becoming less and less domestic. I put a pebble back
in the ground because I took it out as I was turning because it felt right.
It turns out it wasn't a pebble at all.
It was a tree-shaped stone. Small and distinct.
I went inside and watched the top of a clock become concrete.
And there I was. And there I threw everything I could think of
at a dartboard on the wall.

# Porching

The baby cries on the ladder in the lawn.  He is blonde.
The ladder lies askew across the lawn flatwise.  Left from work.
Amongst its regular accouterments, is the lawn.  Its red wagon.
Its low hung swing gleaning the grass from a bending
juniper.  Once it is smelled.  Once it specifically.  His mother
comes for him from the porch.  For the baby
in the lawn from the porch.  It is one dozen yards.
From here I am an adjacent porcher.  From here, I learn his name.

# Angler

we ate the sole
we caught near
the river mouth
you said be careful
of the bones
I was

# Newly

where did you come from, small alien
with your alien tools all splayed?

to display my hands
alien consults these fingernails
he approves of

things come swiftly
little rocks at your feet
a spade for trough
how the slow grows
cold on silvery bicycles alien,

it takes so long to approach
what you had meant to do

dell your dimples
deckle your hands
dew your feet
sleep when sleep
that limbo eye
myself might share

you are welcome everywhere
in my house

# Carver

The gourd the children next door made to put on the porch for the neighborhood to see.  Its swill light radiates from center outward.  And what else could you expect from the things that radiate.

Or it was me who made it.  The gourd, that is.  If so, it was me as child in the neighborhood with the knife.  Wristing a spoon.  Also, the knife.

Or it was you.  You, who held the gourd with the knife then spoon.  I will tell you you could.  Might you have slid the knife as one does as a child and pushed through the nearly hollow.  Careful.  Might now the spoon in your hand.  Scraped against.  What flesh it finds.

Splaying the neighborhood with incandescents.

Seeding everything you brought across.

About the sidewalk we walk waiting until the children come out.

# Wet Coat

A woman stood outside the fish fry in her
pea-green pea coat smoking a plastic-tipped cigar.
The ash hung loosely as a close cluster of buntings
gathered round the cloister of a decayed and decaying cathedral.
It fell, diluting into wet sidewalk.  Only beginning to remember
all concrete isn't gray.

Waiting to head back in, for a few minutes she could
do nothing but watch the rain fall on Ingersoll Avenue.
I don't know of anything that happens instantly.
And yet, it is good to think some day's
instance.

The rain and to know you are with her.  Her
and her pea-green pea coat and you think, *No*. You let
yourself believe you have faith.
Faith that thinks yourself into the rain and know.
How she knows you're there.

# Glistener

Listener, it is nice to watch the people go by and the lightning
not overhead but far enough in distance to be careless
of. I like that there is song too. Sometimes one can hear
these songs being sung, even if by the city busses
pushing the air they are just now taking over.
Some nights, I am that bus.

# Sunday

for CAS

The cars had all slipped into their places. Even those still moving
pushed aside the air to stake claim. The disc above athwart the day grew
moving itself elsewhere, so did the shadows beneath the cars
laid out as some ageless organism.

When walking, earlier, four bicycles overtook me. Their tires careered
off the sidewalk and into the grass. New in June. As where the paths
they formed became a circumstance irrevocably.

Motion suits us. When I come back from where I'd left, I place
my shoes on the trunk of an amputated tree. Because I have learned
little about consequence. And night occurs to be nothing
more than a long shadow. I open the door to the porch
with the swinging bench. There I see my shoes made of light
where air pushes a cat beneath a tree. Then my mother
calls just to tell me her lilacs are in bloom.

# Museum

to the greenery room

a box of bamboo to open

a cardboard box for the bamboo

to come to

elsewhere's elsewhere

the room I love in is

things I thought

animal lung in full dimension

billowing cell what's made of us

when I walk

how I'd tell you if I could

how things aren't mountains

sleep on the floor

likening to sound

beneath the fan blading air about this

room with this kind of wall

kind of seed sprouting pot

does one or many

see the four birds at the county line

pass and pass

unbuilt a fence

pick axe and all

we go to a dusty tract

where I jar the dust to grow it

grow it and leave it

there is a tune we could play into

# Grass

*Oh! for a refreshing glimpse of one blade of grass —*
*for a snuff at the fragrance of a handful of the loamy earth!*
*Is there nothing fresh around us?*
— Herman Melville, from *Typee*


We abandon out of lack as much

as want. The trees, too, take to our stays.

To take you to the sea and lose you there. You passed the reef

only you can see. The sea eludes

me and so I hold it in what brain.

Everyone must build a buoy

for themselves

out of others.

# Coroner

what I had wanted
was a shovel the body feels
a world and everything readily

as what I've taped onto
the wall being tacked
where we were ready for

what I owned was

after the fire we both felt
the room was warm
and went to porch

to see the others
among us

# Florida

I am at a lake at night and there are lights putting light on the lake
the lights come from homes
many of them like the lake
the lake which is man made which I can tell from the fountain
in the center of the lake I now hesitate to call lake
and the light is put there and there are the sounds of night
Florida humid so there is lake in the air
I had packed a lunch I had forgotten at home still sitting on the table
and all I can think is there are so many of us and
why there are so many

# Practitioner

my broke fever
and smell
got on me

to meet
we put the table in the corner to use
its yellow

all I wanted was a thimble of it
up to my neck
where I spoke the practitioner

practitioner says:
*the new moon is the no moon we see though, the moon.*

he offers chart for me
many sequenced dashes triangulating what he thought
we'd sought to see

but my cut
rutted limbs
in need of nourishing

after all
the medic ate
only the dumbest fish

# Ceiling

As we are held in suspension at the outermost peninsula

Our thumbs through each other

As we go sailing in our bobbing turrets looking for glass globes that mark

For fish, remember eyes

As we are near the weeks of littoral drift

As the season goes to end

As a house built to be in the dune near water

As we cut open the water opens

You have me

As we see the angled sail

As we are sailing bobbing

As to take the cut

As we hold the air in our capacity

Even flickering comes past comes past

As the peninsula grows beneath our feet

As our fingernails grow indifferent

As of the ocean, remember how we've done

# Playstronomer

I too
have seen celestial light.
Bodies above.

Geomancy can't be *was*
because it is
form still forming.

Civilizations built on this
celestial light
flickered and moved.

There was a period of time
when it was
the only light

and at times, still
only light.
That, and O—

the things we see it by.

# Metropolitician

Houston
there's so little to do
where even less gets done

yes, I saw the man
cut the window
all gray

you could have
put a hand
through it

# Weather

I miss the rain in the city I hate.

I miss the dog on the interstate. He was dead on my arrival.

I have seen a similar dog. What I can say is already in my mouth. His coat was black. Covered what it touched. It smelled of himself.

I have strayed and kept astray. I have filled a jar. Full foreign air. I will not open it. The world has poisoned.

Myself in the city.
Everything I touch gives off heat.
Shame is a word I ask myself.

# Waterer

I can only wish it was.

Forgetting about the days you've forgotten.

The lizards. Were there six? And how many to the hand?
Would they have come near my hand?
You weren't there. How could I ask you.

When we will realize how we forget we and it mucks.

Don't you remember being
when we got out of the woodwork and into

the machinery works?
Trestles of bridge we look before we cross
becoming iron riveted
or do not and go so.
Mother thought we were lost
but I was only loose a tooth
and as for you, I cannot speak.

But you are my brother.

What I want is sustenance

pushing back.

# Tremorharp

If impenetrable fortress, then the harp will stay inside.
It will lean on its harped angle.  Against my foot, against
the air it will take its motion.  Where no one has seen,
but the earth or some occasioned version of the world
but no, none have seen the center, which fonds itself
outward and if the world, then we quake.  If the world
we quake, and do so with
in it.

# Photographer

the photograph doesn't doubt
it's real

I've put in to canister to agitate its puncture

it will be done soon to roll out
the image we took to dilute to another image

lake bank it was the only image we looked at
not through

if I said it's real
won't it want to

# Film

at first was a shell I broke in a singular continent that became several
its spirals were there still unrecognizable as once is only once
something breaks
there is another we do not see who I traced and was ashamed of my greed

I am because I was rescued by a vanishing point
looking to it is taking it from the vanishing point and holding a piece
as one egret in the strobe of lightning is light is held

flashes as egret then as halflight afterimage
a foreigner preceding a foreigner
with appetite the egret approaches egrets

once we were many with fish in our mouths
if it is for me to say then I can say it but
I isn't until we've witnessed

and come outward as you speak so that I might speak
and you know me

even under this filth

then glows

and lies over now

each parade

# Throughput

we put under the table
only the glossiest things
twills of concrete
a ready throughput
ore of ours
a deft little thing
the mocking mechanism
grows teeth
rather we grow
its teeth

# Triangle

The triangle when drawn.
The first line is arbitrary, or rather it follows no set rules, save that it be a line segment — meaning that it have a distinct beginning and end.
Magnitude is of no concern.
The second line follows an additional rule — that it begin at one of the first line's endpoints.
This is free arcing from a point.
From that point it might extend as angularly free as it can so long as it not continue the first line.
The third can only connect.

# Parascope

I forgot it
I have to bring it in the morning
to bring in
morning

*hush, ocean, hush*

side by side we peering out
on the pier
to be here anymore
so there

I see we go
a line not ours
of sight among universal submarine
thick glass drawing
glow attention to itself so we
see not through but its surface
and are terrified
what we do not see
a broken jug
for catching fish
irrevocable

think waving when we stopped to swim
where you tried
filling your mouth
with sea water
you only knew
once you tried

tired of looking out
mirror lens

bent light
is

let it let us
glisten and here
listen in
until we are fixed

inside the swimming pool:
"final words are so hard to devise"

then, what I say next, like
when you come up for another breath,

because you are swimming for breath

# Public Pool

So I sit here, at the public pool, flipping through
*National Geographic*, and there are images of India.
There are images of women and men in India
Making paper. And there are images of the paper.

The thing I love about collages is the way they separate
the image of the person from the person.
And here I am, at the public pool sunk deeply
in a plastic chair. Everyone here is here.

This is how we recognize the chain-link fence
as a mode of significance. This is how we begin
to see one another. The magazine has me bored.
It feels like there was never a time the images took place.

Or rather, the images happened and no one was there
to witness them. Certainly not these faces.
Not the ones I see at the public pool.

# The High-Dive

We forget backwardly how deep
is the pool.

What you mean is I should invent
and to understand my invention.

A parade of painters, unlimited in their techniques,
carried a banner behind them.
It read: *Things come to us.*
We gave them due credit. We told them they were interesting
and that we were glad that they had come.
Each painter was setting up an alcove
which gave a specific size to the public pool's domain.
One set a painting against a sunny portion of chain-link fence.
He could be overheard, I was told, repeating himself:
*Apples, for a while, will live on branches.*

The signs are sparring in the sky.
The kids are on each others' backs,
the taller ones on the bottom turning through

the shallow end. To make the height most dangerous.
From here I can see the rabbit on the other side of the fence.
In fact, I realize there are several rabbits, the longer I look.
And more distantly is a series of buildings varying in height.

# Airplane

By law, I am an airplane. And there is gravity to resist me exactly. I've learned that all things have gravity. Or all things with mass have gravity and are always trying to pull closer. But there is something else.

Maybe a larger mass, to which I am unaware. Inside me there is a notebook with words. It asks, *What is behind the stars?* It contains a drawing of a head-sized hole. Someone not me brought this notebook with its words and drawing into me. Its mass and mine as a compound mass. The singularities are permanently lost. Mine, its.

There are things, some have said, that have no mass. These mass-less particles, if they can be called that, pass through us — the cockpit, cabin, wings, etc.... not to mention the notebook and the words and drawing inside me. Yes, they pass through the head-sized hole and the seatbacks where some rest their heads. I have not smelled my own insides. I have not smelled the orphan notebook. Come inside and tell me about it. The things pass through us and I believe it. But having no mass leaves me curious about gravity.

The mass-less particles pass through us. They must not have gravity. Emanating outward from their source. Somewhere in the universe. There is the universe, I think. Sometimes people enter me and speak. You might see now, how I get caught up here.

# Airplane

Passenger, welcome. I know how you step the jetway. Passenger, you are forgiven. Take off your shoes. I'll do the same. There is nothing we can do wrong here. You can hold my hand. It is okay to be afraid. This time, where we go, we go together. Hold me when you deplane. As I hold you. Carry back what you'd brought me. Give them elsewhere. Everything must keep moving. Keep moving, passenger.

# Airplane

*Mango, mango, thought Amalfitano, and he closed his eyes.*
— Roberto Bolaño, from *2666*

There is a voice over the heads of the passengers, who are me. Everyone is holding everyone's hand. We are going together to Florida, on what is called me though I do not know why and it seems little more than what we've agreed to.

I am a plane to taxi to takeoff and so we fly together. Let us go there, those who go. Would you be so kind as to pick me up an apple off the floor to polish. I want you to be happy.

We've got nothing to gain over the Atlantic and it looks like every body of water I've seen, which we may parse out in our mapbook to look at and we have so and so with our fingers to the pages marked. This is the atmosphere.

Put me in a room that I'm not accustomed to and then I will learn to eat.

# Astronaut

There is no Houston anymore.
I toured the circumference of everything I could
imagine and it wasn't enough to make me
want less or more.

I know that my legs will be weak when I return.
In fact, all of my muscles will be atrophied from the lessening
of gravitational force.  Most think there is no gravity in the space
between earth and moon.  There is gravity everywhere
there is mass.

Then there is no mass.

There is no mad king
with his knuckles wrapping the red-armed chair in the unraveling.
There is no subject.
No pilot hearing his echo in his mask with his oxygen level stabilizing.
No returning to more native atmospheres.  In this descent, there is not enough
time.  There is only enough
to make us want.

# Astronaut

This pilgrimage.
I have awoken from

when I left
light where I returned.

Here I am, am things.

Of willows lining
the bank of some creek,
calling out
from where I cannot see.
Where we are vulnerable
who see. The willows
calling out.
Must we leave too
of it? The willows
of it? Thinking of them
sprouting out from the bank,
some naked where
deer have gnashed away
at the swellings, too, of it?
Is horizon
as grasses and beetle kill
into

what have we awoken to
to say our name.

# Vocation

There is a gathering of gravestones
across from the graveyard.
In the earth are the
gravestones still
smoothed by the man who smoothes
gravestones.  I imagine there is
a man who buys these stones
for the party concerned.
They choose the smoothed stone
from this man
and purchase.  The man who buys
takes the money from the party,
who are sad or tired or not,
to give to the man who smoothes.
The man who buys gives the stone
to a man he knows at the other end
of town.  This other man practices
his vocation, a rare vocation.
He holds a blade to the stone
with the name in mind.  The name
has been passed down from the party,
given to the man who buys stones
who in turn writes the name for the man
with his vocation.  He holds the name
in mind with the blade in hand to put the name
to the stone. The stone purchased.  Purchased
days ago.  What he holds now
he cuts and knows nothing of the named.

# Acknowledgments

Thank you to the editors of the following journals where many of these poems first appeared: *Blue Earth Review, Boston Review, Denver Quarterly, iO, jubilat,* and *OmniVerse.*

I owe much gratitude to many people who guided me in making these poems. Thank you to Matthew Sage, Tiffanie Sage, Caryl Pagel, Arda Collins, Sara Martin, Jerimee Bloemeke, Mark Levine, Jim Galvin, Jeff Griffin, Nikki-Lee Birdsey, Marius Lehene, Jessie Gaynor, Anna Morrison, Jake Fournier, Chris Schlegel, Sara Deniz Akant, and Dora Malech. A special thank you to Dan Beachy-Quick.

# Other Books from Tupelo Press

See our complete list at www.tupelopress.org